SEASONS *of the* SACRED

SEASONS *of the* SACRED

Reconnecting to the Wisdom
Within Nature and the Soul

LLEWELLYN VAUGHAN-LEE

THE GOLDEN SUFI CENTER

First published in the United States in 2021 by
THE GOLDEN SUFI CENTER
P.O. BOX 456, POINT REYES, CALIFORNIA 94956
www.goldensufi.org

Cover Art: Painting, "Old God," by Angus Hampel,
©Angus Hampel, www.angushampel.com.

ISBNs
paperback: 978-1-941394-46-5
pdf: 978-1-941394-47-2
ePub: 978-1-941394-48-9
kindle: 978-1-941394-49-6

Library of Congress Cataloging-in-Publication Data
Names: Vaughan-Lee, Llewellyn, author.
Title: Seasons of the sacred : reconnecting to the wisdom within nature and
the soul / Llewellyn Vaughan-Lee.
Description: Point Reyes, California : The Golden Sufi Center, 2021.
Identifiers: LCCN 2020019996 (print) | LCCN 2020019997 (ebook)
| ISBN 9781941394465 (paperback) | ISBN 9781941394472 (pdf)
| ISBN 9781941394489 (epub) | ISBN 9781941394496 (kindle edition)
Subjects: LCSH: Seasons--Religious aspects.
Classification: LCC BL590 .V39 2021 (print) | LCC BL590 (ebook)
| DDC   203/.6--dc23
LC record available at https://lccn.loc.gov/2020019996
LC ebook record available at https://lccn.loc.gov/2020019997

Contents

PREFACE

As our world appears more and more out of balance, I have been drawn to return to what is essential, simple, and sacred. This is not to deny the multiple challenges of the present time: accelerating climate crisis, refugees fleeing violence and hunger, social and racial inequality and injustice, and the coronavirus pandemic which in a few short months revealed the fragility of our global systems. But I do sense that also present in this time there is a thread to follow that can reconnect us with our roots in the deeper cycles of nature and our own soul. How this can affect our present imbalance and divisiveness I do not know. But it can awaken us to a new story for humanity and the Earth—a foundation for a way of life that is sustainable not just for ourselves but also for the other-than-human world to which we belong—and thus help life return to its inherent natural order and patterns of change, and reveal the love that is the source of all that exists.

—*Llewellyn Vaughan-Lee,*
July 2020

INTRODUCTION

SPIRITUAL ECOLOGY is a recognition that at the root of our present ecological crisis is a spiritual crisis, and that the essence of this spiritual crisis is a forgetfulness of the sacred nature of creation. Our present civilization has become separated from the story of the sacred that belongs to the Earth and our shared existence, that is at the foundation of life itself. As a result we have come to see the Earth as a resource to be exploited and polluted, existing to serve our materialist values, rather than a living being to revere and respect. The work of spiritual ecology is to reconnect with the sacred, so that we can return to a way of life that is in balance with the Earth. This little book weaves poems, images, and stories of the soul together with the greater story of the spiritual nature of the Earth, so that we can rejoin "the great conversation" with the rivers and the forests and the winds and the stars.[1]

There was a time when the language of the Earth was the language of our daily lives, of planting and harvesting, sunshine and storms. The words of the sacred were stars and seeds, mountains and rivers. The soul and the seasons of nature moved together; they spoke the same mystery, the beauty that is within and around us. It was all as natural as breathing, not needing to be remembered because never forgotten. How could you forget the wind on your face or the songs of birds? How could you forget the rise and fall of the tide? These were not stories written in books but lived from morning until dusk, until dreamtime wove another texture into the firelight.

But now we live in a time of forgetting, when the deep resonance between our souls and the soul of the world has been covered over. So there is a pressing need to remember, to recognize this hidden lifeblood of all that exists, its rhythms and movement, and how it makes itself known to us in different ways. We need to relearn how the inner and outer mirror each other, and how to listen to this music, this underlying story. It is, after all, our own story, as well as the story of the Earth, our common home. We can no longer afford to live solely on the surface of our lives, but have to keep open a doorway to this deeper dimension. We need to reconnect the inner and outer worlds that are equally our home, and to be ourselves a connection between them, a place where the heart is always present.

In a recent book, *Spiritual Ecology: 10 Practices to Reawaken the Sacred in Everyday Life*, I gave some simple daily practices for this work of reconnection, including walking, cooking with love, simplicity, and others. The practices I developed over the many years of my own journey have called to me over the seasons of my own soul, speaking in different ways of the unfolding mystery of the sacred, within our psyche and in the world around. This present book includes a collection of poems that have spoken to me similarly. They are meditations on this lived connection, stepping stones to cross from the desolate shores of today's materialistic wasteland, to a different way of being and living.

I offer this small book now, *Seasons of the Sacred*, as a remembrance of how the Earth moves in time, calling us into relationship. As we remember Her, we remember ourselves—who we really are on the level of the soul, repairing the frayed threads between the inner and outer, the part and the whole.

The word "sacred" runs through these pages like a mantra, because it is this essential quality that we vitally need to remember. Hopefully one day we can all recognize that everything we see and touch and feel is sacred, so that this primal note within life can sing again.

THE SACRED

THE SACRED is an essential quality to life. It connects us to our own soul and to the Divine that is the source of all that exists. The sacred can be found in any form: in every drop of dew on an early morning spider's web, in the call of wildfowl at dusk. It speaks to us in a myriad of ways. In my own garden it is in the scent of honeysuckle and the hummingbird drinking nectar, or the chipmunk scurrying after the seeds fallen from the bird feeder. It is also present in every prayer, every song of praise and thanksgiving. The remembrance of the sacred is like a central note within life. Without it something fundamental to our existence is missing. Our daily life lacks a basic nourishment, a depth of meaning.

The "sacred" is not something primarily religious or even spiritual. It is not a quality we need to learn or to develop. It belongs to the primary nature of all that is. When the First

Peoples felt that everything they saw was sacred, this was not something taught but instinctively known. It was as natural as sunlight, as necessary as breathing. We all have within us a sense of the sacred, a sense of reverence, however we may articulate it. It is a part of our human nature.

We each carry this primal knowing within our consciousness, even if we have forgotten it. A relationship to the sacred is older than any formalized religion, even though it lies at the foundation of many religions. It is a fundamental recognition of the wonder, beauty, and divine nature of the world. It is a felt reverence, an inner sense—we even speak of "a sense of the sacred." If we remember the sacred we will find ourself in a world awake in wonder. However we may call this mystery, it permeates all of creation. It may be more easily felt in certain places, in ancient groves, beneath star-filled skies, in temples or cathedrals, in the chords of music. But this is a mystery that belongs to all that exists—there is nothing that is separate from it. As such it celebrates the unity that is within and around us, the living oneness of which we are a part. Our sense of the sacred is a recognition that we are a part of this deeper all-embracing mystery.

The sacred connects the inner and outer world, the physical world of the senses and the world of the soul. What is seen in the outer can also be felt in the inner world, in our prayers and meditations, in our dreams and their symbols. The sacred pervades all that exists. It belongs to our inner as well as outer life. What matters is our recognition of the sacred, because through it we touch the root of our being. Too easily and often the demands of our daily activity rob us of this awareness, keep us caught in surface distractions. And so we are starved of something essential, even if we do not know we are hungry.

The sacred is not something static or easily defined. It belongs to the wonder of life and its deepest meaning. It is also part of the flow of life, its constant change. And yet it has cycles, patterns of meaning. Both creation and the soul have their seasons, their times of light and dark, times of birth, blossoming and abundance, times of fruition, decay and apparent barrenness. It can be helpful to recognize these changing seasons of the sacred. Then we can see how the deeper patterns within our own life follow these rhythms—how we are part of this ever-evolving mystery.

The sacred is within and all around us, and yet it is often hidden from us. In order to experience the sacred within life we need to step out of our rational mind into an older part of the brain, the part that thinks in images rather than words. This older consciousness will give us a greater awareness of the sacred and the numinous inner energy that it radiates. We will sense, feel the presence of, the sacred, as well as see its signs. It is like entering the caves in Lascaux, France, filled with Paleolithic paintings covering the walls: black bulls, stags, a bird, a bear, even a rhinoceros. This is a wonder from a time before the reign of the rational mind, when magic and mystery were alive in symbol and movement.

Stepping into this quality of awareness is like entering a temple or any sacred space that opens the receptivity of the soul. It is this inner receptivity that enables our innate sense of the sacred to come into our awareness. We learn to develop an inner eye that gives us a sensitivity and the deep understanding that comes from our own sacred nature. Black Elk describes this awareness:

> "And while I stood there
> I saw more than I can tell
> and I understood more
> than I saw; for I was seeing
> in a sacred manner the
> shapes of all things in the
> spirit, and the shape of all shapes
> as they must all live together like one being."

The awareness of the sacred is an essential part of our nature, even if we have almost forgotten how to see in this way. The poems and images in this book are offered as a way to help us to reconnect with our own sacred manner of seeing. As a series of meditations on the sacred, they are a glimpse at what is hidden beneath the many forms of creation, in the world around us and under our feet.

SEASONS of the SACRED

THE SACRED is a quality of the soul, of our inner being and the inner being of the Earth. The experience of the sacred follows the rhythms of the soul and of the Earth, the cycles of becoming, the seasons of life. In today's world we are caught in an image of time as an endless flow of minutes, days, and years that never return—a river of time that is always passing. We rarely think anymore of time as cyclical, of the days as a movement of light and dark, or the years as a pattern of returning seasons—most of us do not live on the land with its rhythm of sowing and harvesting. We have also almost forgotten how the outer movement of time can reflect the time of the soul. Few still mark the year with the saint's days, or the prayers, rituals, or dances that belong to sacred days. Nor do we hear the monastery bells that, before the arrival of clocks, divided the day for both the monks and the medieval farmers, a day that began with Matins and ended with Vespers.

This deeper cycle of sacred time that was known to our ancestors linked the greater and lesser events of their lives—the days, the seasons, and the years:

> To every *thing there is* a season, and a time to every
>   purpose under the heaven:
> A time to be born, and a time to die; a time to plant,
>   and a time to pluck up *that which* is planted;
> A time to kill, and a time to heal; a time to break
>   down, and a time to build up;
> A time to weep, and a time to laugh; a time to mourn,
>   and a time to dance;
> A time to cast away stones, and a time to gather
>   stones together; a time to embrace, and a time
>   to refrain from embracing;
> A time to get, and a time to lose; a time to keep,
>   and a time to cast away;
> A time to rend, and a time to sew; a time to keep
>   silence, and a time to speak;
> A time to love, and a time to hate; a time of war,
>   and a time of peace.
>
> *Ecclesiastes* 3:1–8

This deeper rhythm of time is the rhythm of the sacred. To be in the presence of the sacred is to be present in a time very different from what we experience in our rushed days with the constant demands of the clock. It allows us to listen to a rhythm of meaning, understanding our place within patterns of time that link the growth of a seed to the phases of the moon and the movement of the stars. To live in sacred time is to be present in how this greater pattern connects with our own soul, our inner being, in which every breath is a sacred moment.

But despite our forgetfulness, despite our heated or air-conditioned homes and offices, our disconnection from the soil, the seasons still speak to most of us, from the first warm breath of Spring to the cold wind of Winter. The seasons remind us of our deeper roots and the rhythms that are our heritage. As we get older we can also begin to sense the same seasons in the passage of years, from birth and childhood to old age when our body's energy lessens before time returns us to the earth. In the unfolding of our soul we can recognize similar patterns. In previous times and cultures this inner unfolding was marked by initiations, by sacred rites of passage. Now, for most of us there are few outer initiations. Instead, if we pay attention, we can come to feel the seasons that define our own soul. We can learn to respect and appreciate the way time speaks to us, how its wisdom is within us.

The poems and images that weave through this book are separated into different seasons, the different ways the sacred unfolds into our life. Putting aside our daily concerns and our mind's clutter, we can learn to be present to the presence of the sacred in each moment. Every moment is unique, offering its own way to connect to what is deepest within us, to the wonder and mystery of being fully alive.

> Ten thousand flowers in spring, the moon in autumn,
> a cool breeze in summer, snow in winter.
> If your mind isn't clouded by unnecessary things,
> this is the best season of your life.
>
> Wu-Men[2]

SPRING

SPRING is the time of birth and beginnings, from the first shoot pushing up through the softening earth, the first bud breaking into blossom, and the first stirrings of the soul awakening to its true nature. Love also has a springtime, the turning within the heart as heart looks for heart, lover for beloved. The energy of life and love flow through everything, and Spring is the time when it begins to be reborn, to surface from the sleep of Winter.

There is a deep joy in this awakening, the joy that belongs to life itself—life that is sacred. We feel this joy most fully in the birth of a child, that sacred moment when the soul begins its life in our world. Then the cry of the child echoes something within each of us, a blessing being born. But it is also felt in the first flowers, the colors that come again into our lives each springtime, the air filled with the calling of birds. It is a primal recognition of how we are all a part of this great rejoicing oneness we call life. And in this awakening, we reconnect with the sacred—we need this nourishment for the soul. It is all around us, in the seeds and the sun, and yet we need to look, to uncover, to be a part of the wonder of life waking up.

Life and love call to us, and instinctively we respond. We are part of nature, and the rhythms of the soul resonate with what is happening within and all around us. Even in city streets Spring speaks to us like weeds pushing through concrete, calling to us, reminding us of the simple wonder and joy of being alive, of rebirth. If we listen carefully we can hear how this call comes from the outer world and also from our soul and the soul of the world—it is a mystery that starts to sing. Our work is always to respond, to be present and attentive to this miracle of outer and inner rebirth. Each moment of awakening, of birth, is a gift, a grace we are given.

We all have our treasured moments when the sacred first spoke to us. For some it was all around in the joy, laughter, and secrets of childhood, when our hearts still remembered the light from which we had come. We had not yet forgotten and this inner essence was the most natural of friends. The invisible world was not fully separate and magic was present. Our toys and unseen friends spoke to us and we had not yet learned to forget. Yet many others missed those early years, never knew this simple sunshine in which everything was alive.[3] Then, one day, when the clouds part, our first glimpse of the sacred is something unexpected and wonderful. It is like falling in love, or waking after a troubled dream. How could we have known what we had been missing, what joy was waiting? And now, in an instant, this laughter is with us:

> Sudden in a shaft of sunlight
> Even while the dust moves
> There rises the hidden laughter
> Of children in the foliage
> Quick now, here, now, always—[4]

This is the moment that is always alive, the moment that speaks to us with the intensity of what is, the moment when the sun breaks through and we remember why we are here.

> And the pool was filled with water out of sunlight
> And the lotos rose, quietly, quietly,
> The surface glittered out of heart of light ...[5]

The tragedy is when we miss this moment, when we sleep through this season of awakening, or do not recognize what we have been given. This first season of the sacred is always a gift, but we have to be present to receive it, and then to treasure what we have been given. The sacred requires a quality of attention and receptivity, and a way to stay with this inner meeting, so that even amidst all the demands of our daily life it is not lost. It is the most natural happening, and yet it requires nurturing, most especially the nurturing or presence of the heart.

Just like anything that belongs to nature, the sacred has to be tended in the right way. Its birth is a miracle, and yet we have to be attentive. We need to make a living relationship that nurtures both the sacred and our self. We have to learn how to listen, to watch, to feel the ways of the sacred. Sadly our present culture has mostly forgotten this inner wisdom, so we have to relearn what was so familiar to our ancestors. But it remains within our memories, within our own soul. Like many aspects of our inner nature, it is just waiting to be remembered and then lived.

We have to be present without interfering, without covering it with our demands or desires. The sacred is not something we possess, but something we revere. In our desire-oriented culture there is the danger that we try to use the sacred to get what we want, to make our surface lives more fulfilled, more meaningful or special. The sacred can give us these qualities, but only in its own ways, and never if we demand. The sacred does not belong to us, and if we try to make it answer our personal needs, it will lose its magic, its connection to the source of life. Nor does it belong to our rational world, with its practical rules and logic, which cannot grasp its numinous energy, the power and meaning that come from our older, pre-rational selves. We cannot force or manipulate the sacred, but if we listen, are attentive and respectful, it will answer our needs in more ways than we can imagine. It has its own magic and mystery.[6]

In this first season of the sacred, when it is being born, first coming into our lives, it is vital that we tend it as carefully as we would any birth, any new shoot or opening bud. We watch, sense its beauty and the miracle that it is giving to us. And we try to stop from interfering. This is the art of "work without doing," the ancient way of working with inner and outer nature:

> Less and less is done
> Until nothing is done.
> When nothing is done, nothing is left undone.
>
> The world is ruled by letting things take their course
> It cannot be ruled by interfering.[7]

SPRING POEMS

Nothing is so beautiful as Spring—
    When weeds, in wheels, shoot long and lovely and lush;
    Thrush's eggs look little low heavens, and thrush
   Through the echoing timber does so rinse and wring
   The ear, it strikes like lightnings to hear him sing;
     The glassy peartree leaves and blooms, they brush
     The descending blue; that blue is all in a rush
  With richness; the racing lambs too have fair their fling.

What is all this juice and all this joy?
    A strain of the earth's sweet being in the beginning ...

GERARD MANLEY HOPKINS

Sitting silently
Doing nothing
Spring comes
And the grass grows by itself.

MATSUO BASHÔ

Behold, my brothers, the spring has come; the earth has received the embraces of the sun and we shall soon see the results of that love!

Every seed is awakened and so has all animal life. It is through this mysterious power that we too have our being and we therefore yield to our neighbors, even our animal neighbors, the same right as ourselves, to inhabit this land.

TATANKA YOTANKA, SITTING BULL

But listen to me: for one moment,
quit being sad. Hear blessings
dropping their blossoms
around you. God.

RŪMĪ[8]

What is this precious love and laughter
Budding in our hearts?
It is the glorious sound
Of a soul waking up!

HAFIZ[9]

My Beloved spake, and said unto me, Rise up my love, my fair one, and come away.

For, lo, the winter is past, the rain is over *and* gone;

The flowers appear on the earth; the time of the singing *of birds* is come, and the voice of the turtle is heard in our land;

The fig tree putteth forth her green figs, and the vines *with* the tender grape give a *good* smell. Arise, my love, my fair one, and come away....

My beloved *is* mine and I *am* his: he feedeth among the lilies.

THE SONG OF SOLOMON[10]

I have no name:
I am but two days old.—
What shall I call thee?
I happy am,
Joy is my name.—
Sweet joy befall thee!

WILLIAM BLAKE[11]

A monk asked the Zen master Fuketsu: "Without speaking, without silence, how can you express the truth?"

Fuketsu observed: "I always remember spring in southern China. The birds sing among innumerable kinds of fragrant flowers."[12]

SUMMER

UMMER is a season of abundance, when the myriad forms of nature are in a profusion of color, fragrance, beauty—grasses growing high and lush, rich jasmine fragrances, and the nighttime cadence of cicadas. Now the buds have become a million leaves. The inner world also has its abundance, when the initial awakening of the sacred becomes dreams filled with symbols, pointing us to the riches and depth of meaning that belong to our psyche. Sometimes the inner and outer mirror each other with synchronicities and symbolic happenings, chance meetings or other unexpected events, that make us aware of the richly textured inner and outer worlds we inhabit. Sometimes this symbolic world arrives through music, painting or dance, or any of the other ways the inner world shares its sacred self. And we are the recipient of these gifts that suddenly make our lives abundant in ways we could never have imagined. The horizons of our world expand, other colors are present, new doors are opened.

When we arrive in this profusion of meanings we feel their wonder, we feel connected, part of an interconnected web of inner and outer bounty. We feel alive in ways we never envisioned, alive not just in the outer world, but in our soul which is now singing. The song of life is the music of the sacred, because *life is sacred*, in all of its forms and symbols. And from the first bud opening we have become part of this flowering, this flow of endless imaginings. The sacred is always alive, mysterious, even full of tricks as it frees us from our imprisoning thought-forms and limited sense of self. The Summer of the sacred is full of magic and possibilities.

And this season is also full of power and energy—the full glare of the sun, its heat sometimes overwhelming. Or the thunderstorms of a Summer afternoon, when the thunder seems so close and the downpour of rain a tumult. This also belongs to the inner world, because although it may be more hidden, the sacred can speak to us with power and passion. It can demand that we recognize its meaning, its purpose. Sometimes it wants to change the direction of our life, or pull us into a relationship that speaks to our soul. Sometimes it just wants us to be more fully alive, less trapped in our mind or personality. There are so many ways the sacred speaks to us, sometimes softly, a whisper hardly heard, or a voice calling our name in a dream, or a demand that will not be denied.

Sometimes the sacred arrives and pulls at our hand like a lost child, needing to be taken home. It can come like a lover wanting us, or a symbol that suddenly catches our attention. In our culture we tend to forget that the sacred is alive and does not belong to our surface self, or follow the rules that we have created. It belongs to an inner realm more ancient and wise than our rational mind, like a tree that has grown for centuries, its roots spread out in the forest.

When the sacred is alive and abundant, and we feel its power and pull, it is wise to embrace it as fully as we can. We can recognize when something is sacred because it speaks to a part of us that is normally hidden. But then to respond requires vulnerability and openness, an acceptance of something so much deeper and older than our ego or mind. This is the world from which myths are born, that can take us into this dimension of our self. There was a time when everything in outer life was sacred, from sowing and plowing to cooking and sharing food. In this world we knew where we belonged, from the depths of our soul to the rituals of daily life. Everything was a part of a meaningful whole, in which every individual life was part of a sacred story. We have lost this way of life—our present culture is disconnected from its roots in the inner. But the sacred can still connect us to an inner life that supports and nourishes us. It can bring back magic and wonder and mystery, and a sense of once again being part of a living whole. This is like the life we see around us in a forest or a field: flowers and grasses and insects and birds, all interconnected—colors, sounds, fragrances—communicating, sustaining each other in hidden ways.

The sacred itself cannot be bought or sold. It is not a commodity, even though today people may try to market it. It is a force of life, sometimes seemingly insignificant, but its power comes from its connection to the depths and its divine nature. There are so many signs of the sacred, so many ways to notice and follow it. Each atom in creation is alive with its hidden light, each particle comes from this same source. Do we dare to be fully alive in a world we cannot master or control? Do we dare to say "yes" to the passion of our soul, to an invisible world that calls to us through what is visible? Are we able to be present to what is, rather than what we want or imagine?

In all of its forms the sacred draws us back to the source, to our own wholeness and to the oneness that is love. There are so many words for the same essence that is within everything, that gives life its spark, that makes our heart warm. The lover gives herself to love, the gardener to the mystery of growing and the potency of the soil. The mystic is drawn more and more deeply into prayer. It is all One, calling to us to remember, to reconnect, to sense the sweetness that is all around us. The sacred needs our participation; otherwise its purpose remains unfilled, its wine not drunk. Summer is the time to give our self completely, to allow the abundance of the soul to become part of our everyday life. We have to taste life fully. This season will not last forever, even if it can connect us to what is eternal. We have to live this season with the generosity of our own hearts, our own giving of our self.

SUMMER POEMS

There isn't a particle in creation
that doesn't carry your Light
yesterday I was asking others for a sign of You
today there isn't a sign that isn't of You

JAMI

When the fragrance of the I am He is upon the wind,
The bee of the heart finds the flower of its choice,
And nestles there, caring for no other thing.

KABIR

Every particle of the world is a mirror
In each atom lies the blazing light
   of a thousand suns.
Cleave the heart of a rain-drop
   a hundred pure oceans will flow forth
Look closely at a grain of sand
   the seed of a thousand beings can be seen ...
Within the pulp of a millet seed
   an entire universe can be found.
In the wing of a fly
   an ocean of wonder;
In the pupil of the eye, an endless heaven.
Though the inner chamber of the heart is small,
   the Lord of both worlds
   gladly makes His home there.

MAHMUD SHABISTARI

i thank You God for most this amazing
day:for the leaping greenly spirits of trees
and a blue true dream of sky;and for everything
which is natural which is infinite which is yes

(i who have died am alive again today,
and this is the sun's birthday;this is the birth
day of life and of love and wings:and of the gay
great happening illimitably earth)

how should tasting touching hearing seeing
breathing any-lifted from the no
of all nothing-human merely being
doubt unimaginable You?

(now the ears of my ears awake and
now the eyes of my eyes are opened)

E. E. CUMMINGS

For all things
sing you: at times
we just hear them more clearly.

RILKE

Tie yourself to everything in creation
That got poured from God's magic hat.

O, tie your soul like a magnificent sweet chime
To every leaf and limb in existence ...

HAFIZ[13]

A fish cannot drown in water,
A bird does not fall in air.
In the fire of creation,
God doesn't vanish:
The fire brightens.
Each creature God made
must live its own true nature;
How could I resist my nature,
That lives for oneness with God?

MECHTILD OF MAGDEBURG

You've traveled up ten thousand steps
in search of the Dharma.
So many long days in the archives,
copying, copying.
The gravity of the Tang and the profundity
of the Sung make heavy baggage.
Here! I've picked you a bunch of wildflowers.
Their meaning is the same
but they're much easier to carry.

HSU YUN[14]

AUTUMN

AUTUMN is the season of fruition. It is the time when the fruit ripens on the tree, when the apples, pears, the grapes all sweeten. Those who live the inner life of the sacred also have a season of maturing, when the understanding that comes from the soul bears fruit. There is a quality of wisdom that comes from a lived relationship to the sacred, that belongs to the moment and yet is born through time. For Indigenous Peoples this knowledge was held by the elders, while in today's culture it can belong to anyone whose perception has become deeply familiar with the ways of the sacred.

Sadly the instantaneous nature of today's fast-moving world rarely allows for the patience needed for this depth of awareness, this way of waiting for the inner to unfold into life and express itself. We are too caught in the distractions and demands of each moment that rushes by to have the patience to "wait until the water settles and the right answer arises by itself." But this is the way the sacred unfolds, and we need to learn to sit with it, just as we would wait for a fruit to ripen on the bough. If we pick it too early there is only a sour taste, but if we wait until the moment is right, then there will be a sweetness, a quality of understanding that comes when something is ripe. There is great wisdom in allowing things to take their natural course, to fulfill themselves in their own time, according to their own rhythm.

From this time of inner fruition comes an understanding of how the sacred pervades everything, how it is within and around all of creation. It is at the core of each single thing, every atom that exists, and yet it is also a greater presence, a substance that binds each part into the greater patterns that hold the meaning of the whole. It is as if the sacred is in each single note and yet is also the entire symphony of life's purpose. Only from a place of maturity, and the detachment that comes with time, can we hear what is within the particular and the whole, the many threads and the woven fabric of life.

Autumn is the season when these inner mysteries come to the surface to make themselves known. By now we should have learned the language of the sacred, be in harmony with its ways. We should feel what it is saying and be responsive to its rhythm, our heartbeat aligned with this pulse of life. We are a part of the sacred and it is a part of us—it belongs to our real nature. It is only the disconnection of our culture, its fundamental forgetfulness, that has isolated us within our own individual ego-self, seemingly separate, struggling, unsupported by this basic energy and power within creation. Once we have learned to walk in a sacred manner, our feet touching the earth, we honor this connection that links our soul to the world soul, our breath to the breath of the spirit, that reveals our individual story as a part of the Earth's story.

This greater understanding is not complicated. We live in an age that values complexity, but the sacred enables us to see the simple in what appears complex, because it returns us to the essence, to the root, to the spiritual core of what exists. It is the connection that binds everything together in the inner, that gives life its wonder and numinous beauty. It is what enables the created world—the rivers and stones, the rain and the sunlight—to speak to our soul.

And when we return to this root we find the still center, the innermost home of the sacred and the home of our soul. As the energy of life follows the cycle of the seasons, it brings us to this center, this sacred space, the heart, which is so small and yet contains the infinite and all that exists. Everything is born from a seed and returns, and the journey of the sacred is this return journey. And within this center love is waiting, because love is the secret within our hearts and the heart of the world. Love is the calling of the wind and the stars and the daisy turning towards the sun. Love is creation's greatest promise and most simple essence. Love is the sweetness of the fruit that is ripe and the mystery of life.

AUTUMN POEMS

        For I have learned
To look on nature, not as in the hour
Of thoughtless youth, but hearing oftentimes
The still, sad music of humanity,
Nor harsh nor grating, though of ample power
To chasten and subdue. And I have felt
A presence that disturbs me with the joy
Of elevated thoughts; a sense sublime
Of something far more deeply interfused,
Whose dwelling is the light of setting suns,
And the round ocean, and the living air,
And the blue sky, and in the mind of man,
A motion and a spirit, that impels
All thinking things, all objects of all thought,
And rolls through all things.

                    WILLIAM WORDSWORTH

O God
Whenever I listen to the voice of
       anything You have made—
The rustling of the trees
The trickling of the water
The cries of birds
The flickering of shadow
The roar of the wind
The song of the thunder
       I hear it saying

God is One!
Nothing can be compared with God!

RÂBI'A[15]

How can the divine Oneness be seen?
In beautiful forms, breathtaking wonders,
awe-inspiring miracles?
The Tao is not obliged to present itself
in this way.
If you are willing to be lived by it, you will
see it everywhere, even in the most
ordinary things.

LAO TSU

Everything you see has its roots
In the unseen world.
The forms may change
Yet the essence remains the same.
Every wondrous sight will vanish,
Every sweet word will fade,
But do not be disheartened,
The Source they come from is Eternal,
Growing, branching out,
Giving new life and new joy.
Why do you weep?
That source is within you
And this whole world
Is springing up from it.

RŪMÎ

The thief
Left it behind—
The moon at the window.

RYÔKAN[16]

Lately I became aware of the meaning of Quietude.
Day after day I stayed away from the multitude.
I cleaned my cottage and prepared for the visit of a monk
Who came to me from the distant mountains.
He descended from the cloud-hidden peaks
To see me in my thatched house.
Sitting in the grass we shared the resin of the pine.
Burning incense we read the sutras of Tao.
When the day was over we lighted our lamp.
The temple bells announced the beginning of the evening.
Suddenly I realized that Quietude is indeed Joy,
And I felt that my life has abundant leisure.

WANG WEI[17]

As great as the infinite space beyond is the
space within the lotus of the heart. Both
heaven and earth are contained in that inner
space, both fire and air, sun and moon,
lightning and stars. Whether we know it
in this world or know it not, everything is
contained in that inner space.

THE CITY OF BRAHMAN
THE CHANDOGYA UPANISHAD

I saw that He is to us everything that is good and comfortable for us: He is our clothing because love wrappeth us, claspeth us, and all encloseth us with tender love, that he may never leave us; being to us everything that is good.

And He showed me a little thing, the quantity of a hazel-nut, in the palm of my hand; and it was as round as a ball. I looked thereupon and thought; "What may this be?" And I was answered thus: "It is all that is made." And I marvelled how it might last, because it was so small. And I was answered: "It lasteth and shall ever last for that God loveth it. And everything hath being by the love of God." And in this little thing I saw three properties. The first is that God made it, the second that God loveth it, the third that God keepeth it. He is the maker, the keeper, the lover. Yet I cannot know this fully until I am united with Him, until there is nothing between my God and me.

We seek here to have rest in this world where there is no rest. But He is the very rest, and He willeth it to be known and it pleaseth Him that we rest in Him. We will never rest until we leave this world and are with Him that is all, then the soul is able to receive spiritual rest.

JULIAN OF NORWICH

WINTER

ND FINALLY we are taken into Winter, when the leaves are fallen from the trees and the branches are bare. Winter is this barrenness that belongs to what is essential. Even the colors of Autumn have faded, the leaves scattered; the sound of the animals muted. The cycle of the sacred that began with a spark, a birth and opportunity, changed into the many forms, colors, fragrances—all the possible variations and many possibilities of the inner and outer life. Then after the season of Autumn comes the way the sacred returns from form to the formless. This is the return to the essence of life, which is the breath of the soul, the inner existence of the heart. It is fully alive and whole without color or fragrance, without sound. This season of Winter is a time of completion.

Our present culture is not inclined to value this final season, as if we are reluctant to follow the natural cycle of the seasons, reluctant to allow the world to be laid bare. We seem to want to remain in a perpetual Summer, a time of abundance, without continuing to this completion. It is as if we are frightened by the apparent barrenness of Winter, the in-breathing of life, when what has been born returns to its essence. But without this part of the cycle we would remain trapped in the play of forms, without acknowledging the mystery of the formless and its part in the cycle of life. Forms and the formless belong together, just as expansion and contraction bring balance and harmony.

Perpetual expansion is like the myth of constant economic growth, something that cannot be sustained and is not natural. All things need to return to the ground of their being—the out-breath needs to be followed by the in-breath. This is a time when action becomes non-action, sound becomes silence. We see the essence in things, within our self and within the world. It can be a time when we consider what is essential in our own life, and what needs to fall away or be left behind. The ability to let go is a wisdom that belongs to Winter.

We should not be frightened of this time of seeming contraction—it belongs to the inner way of the sacred and also to the cycle of nature. Each season has its purpose, its beauty and wonder; what Winter offers is a landscape covered in the bright pure white of snow—an expanse of light without distortion or distraction. Love too has its Winters: times of desolation, when love strips us bare, when its wind leaves us cold, seemingly abandoned. It is rarely easy to step into this other, to leave behind what we have accumulated, to make this transition. We are easily caught in all the possessions and attachments that have filled our days.

Sometimes age naturally takes us into this space, as the body or the mind no longer has the energy to accumulate or to hold on to what we have. For some this space comes without struggle, a natural letting go. Some people are more easily present in a life without definition, with the naturalness of what appears empty, while others fight this dying, this apparent losing. Sadly, in our culture dying can seem like failure—we lack the wisdom of letting things die. But we all need to recognize the sacred dimension of this shift, this welcoming of what is without form.

> The ten thousand things are born of being
> Being is born of not-being.[18]

This is a season of completion, when all that has been experienced in the abundance of form completes its journey, discovers its deeper significance. Without this space the sacred would lack a foundation. This is when we "take upon us the mystery of things." We become the space where form and the formless meet, where the heart is empty and full and love opens the door between the worlds. Life and death belong together in ways we rarely understand. Death is not just the end of the cycle of life, but a deepening of the journey. Completion is a realization, not just a conclusion.

And yet it needs an inner strength to fully honor this cycle of the sacred, to allow life's book to turn to this empty page. We have to acknowledge that we are a part of a greater whole than we can imagine, a whole that includes the formless as well as the multitude of forms. Hopefully during the cycle of the seasons we have learned this strength—hopefully the sacred has taken us to this place where we are no longer frightened by the unknown. The wisdom of the sacred is in how it can give us what we need for each stage of the journey. Otherwise we are left stranded, unable to take another step. This is part of the tragedy of our present culture, whose disconnection with these deeper rhythms leaves so many people stranded, without the substance of the sacred, without having developed the qualities needed to complete the journey. How can one go further without welcoming Winter, knowing it will be cold and have an element of desolation, but also sensing the beauty of this bareness?

Few words can be said of where this cycle finally takes us. But in the pattern of the seasons there is a simple mystery: after Winter comes Spring—there is another birth, as the light in the midst of darkness takes us further on the journey of no end. "Letting the breath come and go, we die and live, night and day, winter and spring!"—And the final image of an empty circle contains both the cycle of form and the formless.

WINTER POEMS

one winter afternoon

(at the magical hour
when is becomes if)

a bespangled clown
standing on eighth street
handed me a flower

Nobody,it's safe
to say,observed him but
myself;and why?because

without any doubt he was
whatever (first and last)

mostpeople fear most:
a mystery for which i've
no word except alive

—that is,completely alert
and miraculously whole;

with not merely a mind and a heart

but unquestionably a soul—
...

E. E. Cummings[19]

What legacy shall I
Leave behind?
Flowers in spring.
Cuckoos in summer.
Maple leaves in autumn.

RYÔKAN

Practice non-action.
Work without doing.
Taste the tasteless.
Magnify the small, increase the few.
Reward bitterness with care.
See simplicity in the complicated.
Achieve greatness in little things.

LAO TZU—63

We two alone will sing like birds i' th' cage.
When thou dost ask me blessing, I'll kneel down
And ask of thee forgiveness. So we'll live,
And pray, and sing, and tell old tales, and laugh
At gilded butterflies, and hear poor rogues
Talk of court news, and we'll talk with them
too—
Who loses and who wins, who's in, who's out—
And take upon 's the mystery of things
As if we were God's spies.

SHAKESPEARE, *KING LEAR*

I said to my soul, be still, and let the dark come upon you
Which shall be the darkness of God. As, in a theatre,
The lights are extinguished, for the scene to be changed
With a hollow rumble of wings, with a movement of
      darkness on darkness,
And we know that the hills and the trees, the distant
      panorama
And the bold imposing facade are all being rolled away—
Or as, when an underground train, in the tube, stops
      too long between stations
And the conversation rises and slowly fades into silence
And you see behind every face the mental
      emptiness deepen
Leaving only the growing terror of nothing to
      think about ...

T.S. ELIOT

That we may merge into the deep and dazzling
darkness, vanish into it, dissolve in it forever in
an unbelievable bliss beyond imagination, for
absolute nothingness represents absolute bliss.

GREGORY OF NYSSA

In the beginning there was nothing,
 nor was anything lacking.
The paper was blank. We pick up the paint brush
 and create the scene ...
The landscape, the wind whipping water in waves.
Everything depends upon the stroke of our brush.
Our Ox lets the good earth lead it,
Just as our brush allows our hand to move it.
Take any direction, roam the world to its
 farthest edge.
All comes back to where it started ...
 to blessed Emptiness.

HSU YUN[20]

Here, Sariputra, form is emptiness and the very
emptiness is form; emptiness does not differ
from form, form does not differ from emptiness;
whatever is form, that is emptiness, whatever
is emptiness, that is form, the same is true of
feelings, perceptions, impulses and consciousness.

BUDDHA, HEART SUTRA

RETURN to the SACRED

THESE "seasons of the sacred" are a journey into a deepening relationship with the sacred, with its rhythms and cycles, reconnecting us with this essential quality within our soul and within the Earth. Without this relationship something within our daily life is missing—a quality of meaning is lacking. And yet we have almost forgotten about this ingredient, neglected our relationship to the sacred and to the Earth Herself. And so, unknowingly, we live in an increasingly barren world in which an essential note of life and basic nourishment of the soul are becoming less and less accessible.

Strangely, it appears that while we are becoming increasingly aware of our outer environmental crisis, we hardly notice this inner impoverishment. We are surrounded by more and more distractions that demand more and more of our time and attention. Our computers and smartphones devour us, the images of consumerism addict us. Also our way of thinking—the consciousness with which we perceive the world—has been conditioned to only value the rational mind; we have dismissed the value of our older holistic mind, the part that thinks in images rather than words. It is this older, prerational consciousness that knows the value of the sacred, and can perceive and relate to it both in the symbolic world and in the apparently ordinary things of life. This is the part of our mind that tells stories and remembers myths, being receptive to their deeper meaning without demanding to analyze or dissect. This is also the part of our consciousness that can sit with an image and allow it to speak to our soul, to reconnect us with a deeper part of our self and the Earth and Her primal wisdom.

Our soul is what is most precious within us. It is what gives real meaning and purpose to our existence. The sacred belongs to our soul and the soul of the world and it needs to be nurtured, to be related to with care and love. Care for the soul needs to include care for the sacred, for without it we will become lost without even knowing that we are lost. And care for the Earth needs to combine these two, so that the real music of creation can be heard amidst all the noise of today.

A journey to the sacred is always a return journey, a reconnection with something that is simple and essential within us. This is the light, the beauty, the magic that belong to our soul and also to life itself. It is for each of us to make this journey, to hear this music, this inner heartbeat. And yet it is also the journey of life itself—the great calling that is in the song of every bird, the movement of every cloud, the fragrance of every flower. And now that the Earth is crying out to us, this calling is also painfully present in the images and stories of the destruction of the natural world and its dangerous imbalance, and in the grief that we feel for what is being lost. We are not separate—this is a dangerous story of the last era—but a part of life, and our journey back to the sacred is also life's journey, just as our forgetfulness of the sacred is also life's sorrow. Hopefully the poems and images in this small book can help on this journey, be signposts along a road that is in danger of being forgotten.

Once we reconnect with our innate relationship with the sacred we will find that life will speak to us as it spoke to our ancestors. We will rediscover we are part of a world that is as whole as it is holy, and whose story needs to be heard. We will rediscover how we belong to this sacred story of life, and will again find the deepest meaning in the simplest, most ordinary things.

EPILOGUE

THIS LITTLE BOOK describes the seasons of the soul and places our own individual journey within the greater rhythms of nature, calling for reflection on what we have lost, a simple resonance that carries with it a sense of belonging.

For many Indigenous People, their life is not just part of the oneness of the natural world, but also its spiritual self, whether called the Great Spirit, or in the language of the Kogi, *Aluna*, the spiritual intelligence within nature. For centuries in the West we have lost that sense of connection, both as a felt reverence, and also as an innate understanding of the greater cycles to which we belong. But within these greater rhythms is a wisdom that we now need in order to live in this time of great dying.

In this moment of our collective destiny when we face the truth of species extinction and climate catastrophe, it is vital that we have a sense of these underlying cycles and their meaning. The Earth, our common home, is in the midst of its sixth mass extinction of plants and animals—the sixth wave of extinctions in the past half-billion years. Called the Anthropocene extinction, this man-made biological annihilation is now a central part of our human story, our collective journey. Whether we deny or accept this story, feel grief or anger or continue to distract ourselves, we are a part of this great dying. Nor do we know into what world we are transitioning, whether it will include social collapse together with extreme drought and storms, fires and rising seas.

In such unprecedented times it can be helpful, even necessary, to step back and have a sense of this story in which humanity has come to play the agent of extinction, of ecocide. Whether through greed, ignorance, or simple inability to conceive of our own self-destruction, we are turning the Earth towards Winter. We are a part of the Earth's story, and as we reconnect with this deeper, ancient understanding, we are more able to be fully present in the season of this present time.

What does it mean to live in the Winter of our world, at the end of an era? How can the patterns of nature and the cycles of the soul help us to connect with the teaching within this present moment, to see what life and the Earth are telling us? Only from this understanding can we gain access to the tools, the spiritual and moral values, that can help the Earth and humanity in this darkening season, and then in the transition from Winter to Spring, to what is waiting to be born.

As I have suggested, Winter is a season that draws us back to what is essential, to the roots that sustain us. As we move into this time of great dying and the unknown future of climate catastrophe, it is crucial that we return to the values that are essential to our human nature—love, care for each other and for the Earth. The simple values of connection, values that place cooperation above competition, can support us during the bleakness of Winter—the end of a civilization built upon exploitation—and take us into a new era, belonging as they do to a shared future with the Earth, a future that can only come from a radical shift in our collective consciousness. If we are to finally step into Spring, it will be as a diverse and socially supportive community in which we belong to each other and to the Earth. These seeds, of interdependence and living oneness, are already present, along with a deepening sense of the mystery of life and the soul that is within and all around us.

Notes

1. Thomas Berry, one of the founding voices offering a spiritual perspective to our ecological crisis, wrote: "We are no longer talking to the rivers and forests, we are no longer listening to the winds and the stars. We have broken the great conversation. By breaking that conversation, we have shattered the universe. All the disasters that are happening now are a consequence of this spiritual autism." From *The Dream of the Earth*.

2. *The Enlightened Heart*, edited by Stephen Mitchell, p. 47.

3. I grew up in a grey middle-class house in which joy and magic were not just absent, but not even known. I had to wait to experience it through the eyes, the play and laughter of my own children, to sense its magic, and then sadly see it passing as they left childhood behind. Why some children are given this most precious yet simple childhood gift, while others never come to know it, is also a mystery. It may be more often found in a tenement than a mansion. I do not think that my parents even knew that it existed. I think it belongs to love, and that where love is present it flowers and flows. Without love there is no soil for joy. But love can be present in so many forms, there is no limit to where joy might show up, to where the wonder of life's springtime might bloom. As another mystical poet said about the joy of Spring, it is "a strain of earth's sweet being in the beginning."

4. T.S. Eliot, "Burnt Norton," Four Quartets.

5. Ibid.

6. *Moshkel Gosha: A Story of Transformation* is a little book I wrote that uses an ancient Persian myth to explore the dangers and possibilities of working together with this inner reality, the correct attitude that is needed.

7. Lao Tzu, *Tao Te Ching*, 48.

8. Trans. Coleman Barks, *Say I am You*, p. 62.

9. Trans. Daniel Ladinsky, *The Gift*, p. 19.

10. *The Song of Solomon* 2:10–16.

11. "Infant Joy," *Songs Of Innocence*.

12. Paul Reps, *Zen Flesh, Zen Bones*, p. 138.

13. Trans. Daniel Ladinsky, *The Gift*, p. 265.

14. "Searching for the Dharma," *Six Poems by Hsu Yun*, see www.hsuyun.org.

15. Trans. Charles Upton, *Doorkeeper of the Heart*, p. 48.

16. Trans. R. H. Blyth, *Zen in English Literature and Oriental Classics*, p. 298.

17. *The Mystic Vision: Daily Encounters with the Divine*, compiled by Andrew Harvey and Anne Baring, p. 143.

18. Lao Tzu, *Tao Te Ching*, 40.

19. E. E. Cummings, "one winter afternoon," *73 poems*.

20. Master Hsu Yun, *Poems on the Oxherding Series*.

Acknowledgments

For permission to use copyrighted material, the author gratefully wishes to acknowledge: Alfred A. Knopf, an imprint of the Knopf Doubleday Publishing Group, a division of Penguin Random House LLC, for permission to quote "Verse Forty," "Verse Forty-Eight," and "Verse Sixty-Three" from the *Tao Te Ching* by Lao Tsu, translated by Gia-Fu Feng and Jane English, translation copyright © 1972 by Gia-Fu Feng and Jane English, copyright renewed © 2000 by Carol Wilson and Jane English, all rights reserved; Charles Upton for permission to quote from *Doorkeeper of the Heart: Versions of Rabi'a*, by Rabi'a al-Adawiyya and Charles Upton, copyright © 1988 by Charles Upton, www.charles-upton.com; HarperCollins Publishers, for permission to quote from "Ten thousand flowers in spring..." by Wu-Men, from *The Enlightened Heart: An Anthology of Sacred Poetry*, edited by Stephen Mitchell, copyright © 1989 by Stephen Mitchell; Hohm Press for permission to quote from *This Heavenly Wine: Poetry from the Divan-e Jami*, by Nooreddin Abdurrahman Ibn-e Ahmad-e Jami, renditions by Vraje Abramian, copyright © 2006 Vraje Abramian; Houghton Mifflin Harcourt Publishing Company for permission to reprint excerpts from "Burnt Norton" and "East Cocker" from *Four Quartets* by T.S. Eliot, copyright © 1936 by Houghton Mifflin Harcourt Publishing Company, renewed 1964 by T.S. Eliot, copyright © 1940 by T.S. Eliot, renewed 1968 by Esme Valerie Eliot, all rights reserved; Jane Hirshfield for permission to quote "A fish cannot drown in water," by Mechtild of Magdeburg, translation copyright © Jane Hirshfield, from *Women in Praise of the Sacred* (NY: HarperCollins, 1994); Jonathan Star for permission to quote from *Two Suns Rising: A Collection of Sacred Writing*, copyright © 1991 by Jonathan Star; Liveright Publishing Corporation for permission to quote "i thank You God for most this amazing," copyright © 1950, 1978, 1991 by the Trustees for the E. E. Cummings Trust, copyright © 1979 by George James Firmage, and "one winter afternoon," copyright © 1960, 1988, 1991 by the Trustees for the E. E. Cummings Trust, from *Complete Poems: 1904-1962* by E. E. Cummings, edited by George J. Firmage; Riverhead, an imprint of Penguin Publishing Group, a division of Penguin Random House LLC, for permission to quote "Du kommst und gehst.../You come and go..." by Rainer Maria Rilke, from *Rilke's Book of Hours: Love Poems to God by Rainer Maria Rilke*, translated by Anita Barrows and Joanna Macy, translation copyright © 1996 by

Artwork Acknowledgments

To reproduce copyrighted material, the author gratefully wishes to acknowledge the kind permission of:

About the author

LLEWELLYN VAUGHAN-LEE, Ph.D., was born in London in 1953 and has followed the Sufi path since he was nineteen. In 1991 he moved with his family to Northern California and founded The Golden Sufi Center (www.goldensufi.org).

Author of several books, he has specialized in the area of dreamwork, integrating the ancient Sufi approach to dreams with the insights of modern psychology. Since 2000 the focus of his writing and teaching has been on spiritual responsibility in our present time of transition, an awakening global consciousness of oneness, and spiritual ecology (www.workingwithoneness.org). He has been interviewed by Oprah Winfrey on *Super Soul Sunday*, and featured on the *Global Spirit* series shown on PBS.

About the publisher

THE GOLDEN SUFI CENTER publishes books, video, and audio on Sufism and mysticism. A California religious nonprofit 501(c)(3) corporation, it is dedicated to making the teachings of the Naqshbandi Sufi path available to all seekers.

THE GOLDEN SUFI CENTER
P.O. Box 456 · Point Reyes Station · CA · 94956-0456
tel: 415-663-0100 · fax: 415-663-0103
www.goldensufi.org